The Story of the
MAYFLOWER
COMPACT

Norman Richards

Illustrations by Darrell Wiskur

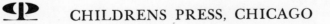

CHILDRENS PRESS, CHICAGO

Library of Congress Catalog Card Number: 67-22901
Copyright © 1967, Childrens Press, Inc.
All rights reserved. Printed in the U.S.A.
Published simultaneously in Canada

6 7 8 9 10 11 12 13 14 15 16 17 18 19 20 21 22 23 24 25 R 75

Seventeen-year-old William Bradford walked through the soft green meadows of Yorkshire, England one fine spring day in 1607. He was on his way to his two uncles' house, where he had lived since his parents died. His father had left him some good land, which he would own when he became twenty-one. In the meantime, his uncles were taking care of it for him.

"Where have you been?" his Uncle Robert asked as he opened the door. "We didn't see you at church today, William."

"I went to the Separatist church service, Uncle Robert," he answered.

"That is not a church service," his Uncle Thomas said sternly. "You know very well that King James has forbidden the Separatists to hold services in churches. They must meet in a barn, like outlaws. The King only allows one church in this country —the Church of England."

6

The King believed that he ruled the people by Divine Right, and that no one could question his actions. He made the laws, and people had to obey them. He appointed the bishops of the Church of England, and they in turn appointed the pastors in each church. The people had to worship in the manner of that church and observe its rules.

Most of the people obeyed the King. They worshiped as he said they must. But some proud, hardworking farmers believed that every man should be free to worship God as he wished. They did not agree with the practices of the King's church. They wanted to worship in a simpler way. They also wanted the right to choose their own pastors to lead them. They decided to separate from the Church of England, and after that they were known as Separatists.

King James did not like the idea of men deciding things for themselves and choosing their own leaders. If they could do this in religion, they would soon demand the same rights in government. He decided to harass the Separatists and make their lives so difficult that they would move away from England. He raised their taxes and had them arrested for the slightest offense against his laws. Citizens who were members of the King's church scorned and insulted the Separatists.

KING JAMES I (1603–1625)

Young William Bradford believed the Separatists were right, but his two uncles were horrified that he would join such an unpopular group. They were afraid he would be arrested and have his land seized by the King's tax collectors.

"Give up this idea of worshiping in another church. Then you can live in peace in your family home and be a prosperous farmer," they told him. "If you don't, you will be driven out of the country without a penny to your name."

"I cannot accept the King's religion," William declared. "I must be free to choose my own way to worship God."

"But the King demands it!" his uncles insisted. "Do you set yourself above your master?"

"No man is my master!" William replied. "I will accept the King as the ruler of my country. I will pay my taxes and do my duty as a citizen. But I will not kneel before him as my master, and I will choose my own religion."

"You have no choice," his Uncle Robert said. "The government and the church are one. That is the way it always has been."

"We Separatists believe the government and the church should be separate," William said firmly, "and that is the way we will have it, even if we must move to another country."

Soon afterward, William met with some of the older leaders of the Separatists, including William Brewster, Edward Winslow and John Carver. They decided that their group must leave England, even though it meant leaving their homes and property.

"Where can we go, to find freedom of religion?" one of them asked.

"Holland is not far away, and the government there will allow us to worship as we choose," William Brewster said.

Early in 1608 they made plans to move to Holland. Not long afterward the families of the group climbed aboard a ship and set sail across the English Channel to their new home. They were saddened to leave their home country, but none of them hesitated. Their people, most of them farmers, did not feel at home in the busy, noisy city of Amsterdam.

They moved to the small town of Leyden.

The group was accepted by the kindly Dutch people, and most of them found work so that they could earn enough money to live. They had to accept the lowest paying jobs, and most of them had to learn new skills. But they did not complain, for they were happy to be free to worship in their own way.

For eleven years the Separatists lived among the Dutch people. Their children played with Dutch children, and learned to speak their language. They skated with their Dutch friends in the winter. They wore wooden shoes and picked tulips in the summer. Many of the English children began to think of Holland as their home, and they forgot about their homeland.

The fathers and mothers began to worry about this. "We are English, and we are proud of our traditions and our people," they said. "The Dutch have been kind to us, but we want our children to be English children. We want them to grow up among our own kind of people."

One night William Bradford, Edward Winslow, John Carver and some of the other leaders had a meeting at William Brewster's house. They had decided to discuss the problem and seek the answer to it.

"Things are even worse for Separatists in England," John Carver said. "Many of those who believe as we do are still living there, but most of them have been thrown into prison. We can't go back there."

"Then where *could* we move, if we want to live among English-speaking people?" William Bradford asked.

"I have been reading about explorers going to the New World in North America," William Brewster said. "There is a colony in Virginia. We could go there and start a colony, too. We would be alone to live and worship as we choose, as Englishmen."

"Where would we get the money for a ship and supplies for such a long voyage?" one of the men asked.

"Some merchants in England will loan us the money for the trip if we agree to pay them back with fish and furs and lumber from the New World," William Brewster replied. "As for King James, he will be glad to grant us permission to go and found a colony, because we will be farther away than ever."

The men voted to go to the New World. It was a daring and dangerous idea. It would be hard for the women and children to live in the wilderness of North America. There were no cities, no houses, and no people to help them. They might starve or be killed by Indians. But their beliefs were more important than having nice houses or lots of food and money. They began to make their plans.

With money provided by English businessmen, the Separatists leaders hired a ship and its crew for the journey across the ocean. The ship was an old one called the *Mayflower*, which had sailed the seas for many years. It was in the harbor at Southhampton, England. It was necessary to buy a small ship, the *Speedwell*, to take the Separatists to England.

They could not all go. There were tears as friends and families said good-bye. It was a fine summer morning in 1620 when the voyagers boarded the little ship. The white sails billowed overhead as the *Speedwell* moved out of the harbor. The men, women

and children aboard waved to their friends standing on the dock. "It was truly doleful," said William Bradford, "but they knew they were pilgrims."

When they reached England, they waited for supplies to be loaded aboard both ships. But the *Speedwell* proved to be leaky. It could not make the trip.

18

"We are going to a land of wilderness," William Brewster said. "We will have to build our homes, weave our cloth, make our barrels and utensils, and defend ourselves in a military way. We do not have many of the necessary skills among us. If we are to succeed with our colony, we will have to bring skilled workmen with us, even though they are not of our group."

The others agreed, and soon skilled workers were volunteering to make the hazardous journey. A professional soldier named Miles Standish was hired to lead the Pilgrims in defending themselves against unfriendly Indians. A cooper, or barrel maker, named John Alden was hired to repair the barrels of fresh water on the ship. An eighteen-year-old girl named Priscilla Mullins joined the group to help mothers with children and cooking. Weavers, hide tanners and carpenters joined the Pilgrims on the *Mayflower*. There were many problems and delays and the summer was slipping away.

Finally, in August 1620, the ship sailed from England. There were 102 passengers and 20 crew members crowded onto the little ship.

Men, women and children had to sleep in the crowded space between the decks. There were no beds, and they had to wear all their clothes to keep warm. There was only a tiny pan of coal in a bed of

sand to cook over, but the women worked hard to cook enough food for everyone. Many times rain and huge waves sent water splashing into the living space. Then everyone had to eat a cold meal of biscuits and salted beef.

THE MAYFLOWER

The Mayflower was a three-masted, double-decked sailing ship.

It was about ninety feet long. It had a twenty-five foot beam (width).

Cargo was stored below the passengers' deck.

Ballast in the depth of the ship helped to hold it upright against the force of the wind on the sails.

The crew lived in the upper section of the ship forward. This is called the forecastle.

The captain lived in the high section above the ship's main afterdeck. There was a galley there where food was prepared.

Sailors sometimes climbed the masts to the crows' nests where they could watch for land or other ships.

After only a few days the *Mayflower* ran into an autumn storm over the Atlantic. The wind howled. Huge waves crashed over the top deck. The little ship tossed and turned wildly from side to side. The Pilgrims were not used to being at sea. They were frightened. But they kept quiet and prayed. Mothers hugged the smaller children and protected them against the wind and waves. The ship's timbers creaked and groaned. Finally, one of the main beams cracked. The men worked quickly to mend it with a large iron screw, and at last the storm passed.

At one point in the storm John Howland was washed overboard. Luckily he caught hold of one of the topsail halyards (a line) and was pulled back aboard.

Afterward, William Bradford remarked, "We did not need a king or a bishop to tell us what to do or how to pray. Each of us did his duty for the good of the whole group."

Most of the passengers thought they were going to a place near Virginia, but the *Mayflower* was headed toward a point farther north. Day after day they sailed on. Winter was approaching, and the weather grew colder and colder.

Then, after sixty-six days of sailing, they spotted a thin strip of land on the horizon. Everyone rushed to the top deck to see it. As the ship drew closer to it, they could see a bleak, sandy shore. There were no hills, no buildings and only a few small trees. They were looking at the tip of Cape Cod, in what is now Massachusetts. The passengers felt discouraged that the land was not prettier, but they were glad to reach the New World.

The next day the ship lay at anchor in a harbor. The passengers were eager to land and start their colony. But some of them who were not members of the Pilgrims worried that the Pilgrim leaders might seize power and force everyone to obey them. They told William Brewster this.

"We came here to escape absolute rule," he said. "We want to choose our leaders, just as we choose our pastors in church."

They decided to write down their ideas so everyone could read them and agree to them or disagree. The men gathered in the largest cabin of the *Mayflower* and talked about their ideas for a government. William Brewster wrote them down on a large sheet of paper. When he had finished, the paper had these words on it:

"In the name of God, Amen. We whose names are underwritten, the loyal subjects of our dread sovereign Lord King James, ... having undertaken for the glory of God, and advancement of the Christian faith, and the honor of our King and country, a voyage to plant the first colony in the northern parts of Virginia, do by these presents solemnly and mutually in the presence of God, and one of another, covenant and combine ourselves together into a civil body politic ... and by virtue hereof to enact, constitute and frame such just and equal laws, ordinances, acts, constitutions and offices, from time to time, as shall be thought most convenient for the general good of the colony, unto which we promise all due submission and obedience..."

This meant that they would consider themselves a group with the right to govern themselves. They would not wait for a king to tell them what their laws were, but would pass their own laws. Everyone who signed the paper agreed to obey the laws of the group.

The agreement came to be known as the Mayflower Compact. Each of the Pilgrim men signed it. They waited for the other passengers who were not Pilgrims to sign it. Miles Standish marched up to the table, his saber at his side, and wrote his name below the others. The rest of the passengers followed quickly.

The Mayflower Compact was an entirely new kind of agreement. Other English colonists had been under the power of a governor appointed by the King. He made the rules and the colonists were forced to obey them without question.

But the Mayflower Compact allowed each man the right to vote and take part in governing himself. They would choose a governor just as the Pilgrims always chose their pastors. If they did not feel that he did a good job of governing, they could elect another man to replace him. John Carver was the first colonial governor elected by the people. When he died after a few months, William Bradford was elected and served as governor for thirty years.

Men had never been allowed to choose their own leaders before in Europe. The Pilgrims had dared to begin a new method of government. Many years later it came to be known as democracy. It was the type of government that the United States of America was to have.

The *Mayflower* sailed on a few miles to a better spot for the settlement. The Pilgrims built their colony there and named it Plymouth, after the city of that name in England.

They lived on the *Mayflower* for three months while shelters were built on the shore. First they built a common house about twenty feet square. Then they built some thatched huts along the brook. By the end of the first year there were seven huts.

The first year was a hard, starving time. Many people died. More would have starved without the help of the friendly Indians. Indians showed the Pilgrims how to plant corn, to find eels and clams, and to get food from the wilderness.

Although the Pilgrims had no serious trouble with Indians they built a fort on the hill. By the end of their second year, an eleven-foot palisade fence enclosed the street of houses and the fort which was used as a church for many years.

In the following years as the colony grew, the Pilgrims put their democratic ideas into use. They held town meetings and voted for their leaders. William Bradford served as a good governor. They passed their own laws and set up schools. In Europe only the wealthy people were allowed to send their children to school, but the Pilgrims believed everyone had the right to be educated. Their children and their grandchildren grew up believing in the ideas written in the Mayflower Compact.

More than 150 years later the American people had become so accustomed to the ideas of democratic government that they wrote them into their country's Constitution. The Pilgrims had hoped that the ideas of the Mayflower Compact would spread to other men, and they did. Governor William Bradford was right when he wrote:

". . . As one small candle may light a thousand, so the light here kindled hath shone unto many, yea in some sort to our whole nation."

30

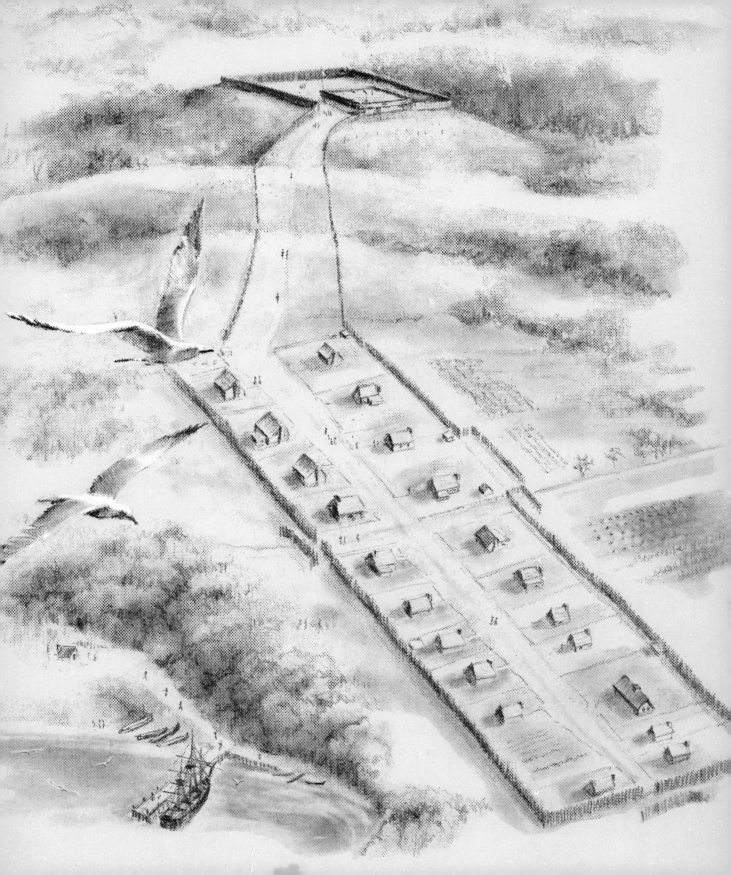

About the author: Norman Richards grew up in a small New England town and developed an early interest in history and transportation. In military and civilian life he has flown in nearly every type of aircraft, including seaplanes, helicopters, amphibious patrol bombers and one of the last surviving dirigibles. A graduate of Boston University's journalism school, Mr. Richards has written more than a hundred articles on aviation and travel. As managing editor of MAINLINER, United Airlines' magazine for passengers, he travels 100,000 miles a year in jets, light planes and helicopters to cover stories.

About the Artist: Darrell Wiskur lives in Aurora, Illinois, with his wife and two small sons. He is a free-lance artist who spends most of his time illustrating books for children. He had his formal art training at the Chicago Academy of Fine Art and at the School of Professional Art. He enjoys hunting and fishing, and his love of nature and the out-of-doors is reflected in his work.